DIARY
OF A
MINECRAFT
CREEPER

Book 1

Creeper Life

by Pixel Kid and
Zack Zombie

Saturday

Hi, my name is Jasper. I'm a Creeper.

And this is my diary.

My mom and dad told me that I bottle up my feelings too much.

They said if I don't let my feelings out that one day I'll explode.

So, they got me this diary to help me chill out.

My whole Creeper village thought it was time to let the world know the truth about Creepers, too.

They thought that I could write something in my diary that would one day set the world straight about Creepers.

I was wondering why they chose me.

Until I realized that I'm the only Creeper that knows how to write.

And, yes, I'm the only Creeper that can write with his feet.

I usually have a lisp when I talk, so I hope you don't mind me hissing sometimes.

Yeah, I'm weird like that.

But at least I'm willing to admith it.

Sorry, there's my lisp again.

HSSSSSSSSS.

So, I wanted you to give you a peek into my diary so you could know what Creeper life is really like.

Thass because most of the things you hear about us are just not true.

Some obsessed Minecraft fans have said things about Creepers that are downright wrong.

Like, I'm sure you've heard that we sneak up on players in Minecraft and blow them up.

Or, that when you're not looking we blow up your house.

Or, that we wait for you to finish your really cool Minecraft creation, which took you weeks to create, all so that we can blow it up.

I just want to let you know that it's not true.

Well. . .not all of it.

Sure, we do sneak up on people. But not on purpose. Most of us are just really shy.

And, sure, we do blow some people up but that's just because we get so excited to meet you that we can't help ourselves.

And, about blowing up your house and your awesome Minecraft creations. . .well. . .that one's true.

We get jealous sometimes because we can't build stuff like that.

It's not our fault. We don't have arms, you know.

Now, you're probably wondering why we blow up when we get excited.

Well, we have this condition. . .and it runs in my family.

You know, like how you have your mom's nose or your dad's unibrow.

Since Creepers are all related, every Creeper suffers from it.

It's called *Spontaneous Combustion*.

Or *Detonitis*, for short.

Don't laugh. It's real.

I'll bet if you looked it up, you would find an article about it online.

Here's an article I found about some doctors who are trying to find a cure for it.

Professor gets crackling on Creeper combustion theory

A CAMBRIDGE professor has tackled the burning issue of spontaneous combustion – using belly pork.

Prof Brian J Ford is a research biologist and author of more than 30 books, most about cell biology and microscopy but he has turned his attention to the mechanisms behind why people 'explode'.

He said in an article in *New Scientist*: 'One minute they may be relaxing in a chair, the next they erupt into a fireball.'

'Jets of blue fire shoot from their bodies like flames from a blowtorch, and within half an hour they are reduced to a pile of ash.

'Typically, the legs remain unscathed sticking out grotesquely from the smoking cinders. Nearby objects – a pile of newspapers on the armrest, for example – are untouched.'

The first record of spontaneous combustion dates back to 1641 when

■ RACHEL ALLEN
Health correspondent

Danish doctor and mathematician Thomas Bartholin described the death of Polonus Vorstius – who drank wine at home in Milan, Italy, one evening in 1470 before bursting into flames.

Since then more reports of spontaneous combustion have been filed and linked to alcoholism – though the link was later disproved.

The most recent case was 76-year-old Michael Faherty who died on December 22, 2010. West Galway coroner Ciaran McLoughlin recorded the cause of death as spontaneous human combustion.

Prof Ford wanted to disprove the alcoholism theory and also something called the 'wick effect' suggested by London coroner Gavin Thurston in 1961.

Thurston had described how human fat burns at about 250c, but if melted it will combust on a wick –

RESEARCH: Prof Brian Ford

such as clothes or other material – at room temperatures.

He wrote: "I felt it was time to test the realities, so we marinated pork abdominal tissue in ethanol for a week.

"Even when cloaked in gauze

moistened with alcohol, it would not burn.

"Alcohol is not normally present in our tissues, but there is one flammable constituent in the body that can greatly increase in concentration."

The body creates acetone, which is highly flammable.

He added: "A range of conditions can produce ketosis, in which acetone is formed, including alcoholism, fat-free dieting, diabetes and even teething.

"So we marinated pork tissue in acetone, rather than ethanol.

"This was used to make scale models of humans, which we clothed and set alight.

"They burned to ash within half an hour.

"For the first time a feasible cause of human combustion has been experimentally demonstrated."

*rachel.allen
@cambridge-news.co.uk*

They say that we blow up because we get so excited that we go through a chemical reaction inside.

Kind of like when you eat too much candy on Halloween and your stomach feels like it's about to explode.

Or if you eat a bad burrito.

So, we do our best to contain ourselves.

But we get excited really easy.

Like, one time my uncle met a really famous celebrity.

He got so excited that when the celebrity was writing him an autograph, my uncle just couldn't hold it in.

It's just a good thing the guy didn't need all his fingers. . .

. . .Or his eyebrows.

Another time, a different uncle of mine found an emerald in an underground cave.

He really did try to contain himself.

But emeralds are just too cool to keep to yourself.

Poor guy. . .

Never made it off the bus.

So, don't think of us as bad.

Creepers aren't bad. We're just easily excitable.

So, if you see us, don't get all crazy and excited.

Because we're really sensitive.

And it probably won't end well. . .for neither one of us.

HSSSSSS.

Sunday

Today, I was wondering where Creepers come from.

So, I decided to ask my mom and dad.

For some reason, they started getting really nervous and started hissing and stuff.

Then they blurted out that Creepers come from monster spawners.

I didn't believe them, though.

Everybody knows that there are no Creeper spawners in Minecraft.

One of the kids from school said that Notch was trying to make a pig but made a mistake and he ended up with a Creeper instead.

I didn't believe him, either.

Creepers don't look anything like pigs.

And I've never heard of a pig spontaneously exploding for no reason.

But if they did, I guess that's what instant bacon would taste like.

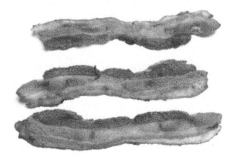

Another kid at school said that Creepers came from a secret military experiment gone wrong.

He said they were trying to make soldiers that could blow stuff up with their minds.

But something went wrong and they ended up with Creepers instead.

He gave me a picture of what we looked like before the experiments.

After seeing it, it kind of made me think that maybe he was right.

Monday

Today, we had a day off from school.

I think it had something to do with a Creeper accidentally walking into the girl's bathroom.

They said it was raining pigtails and makeup all over the place.

Since we had a day off, my family decided to get together for a barbeque.

My whole family was there, including my uncles, aunts and cousins.

But, I don't know. For some reason, every time my family gets together, it seems like there are less Creepers around.

Now, our extended family doesn't get together much.

That's because the last time we tried it, things got really crazy.

Somebody decided it was a good idea to start a food fight.

It didn't end well. . .but the fireworks were awesome!

Now, what's funny is that not all Creepers in my family are green.

Some Creepers are yellow and some are even red.

They say if you're yellow that means if you explode, you make a yellow flame.

And if you're red and you explode, you create a red flame.

But if you're green, all you do is explode.

Yeah, it's not as pretty.

Most of my family live in Biomes with lots of plants.

We can hide better that way.

Though, I heard that a whole group of my uncles, aunts and cousins once moved out west to the desert Biome.

I don't think they thought it through, though.

14

After their first night in the desert Biome, they realized they made a big mistake.

I think it was when they tried to use cactus for pillows.

Yeah, some Creepers aren't the sharpest tools in the Minecraft chest.

Some of my relatives live underground, too. They say that it's a lot safer down there.

But after a while, living in the dark affects your eyesight.

15

I had an uncle once that lived underground for twenty years.

I asked my dad what happened to him.

My dad said that he accidently ran into some Skeletons, who he thought were his relatives.

When he wouldn't stop talking, the Skeletons shot him with an arrow.

Now, all we have left of him is a record of his greatest hits.

Yeah, Creeper families are a real interesting bunch.

We're known for being real sensitive, too.

It doesn't take a lot to get us to our boiling point.

And many of us have an explosive personality.

Also, we're always bursting at the seams with excitement.

So, try not to get us too charged up.

And don't ever, ever, ever try to tickle us.

I mean it.

Tuesday

Today, was my first day back at school.

I was a little bit bummed about it.

Don't get me wrong, my school is really cool.

That's because I go to a school for special mobs.

I tried to go to regular school once, but it didn't go so well.

That's because I have this. . .err. . .problem.

No, not the condition I mentioned to you before.

This is another problem that started happening recently.

You see my farts. . .they're really, really, really bad.

Like, school cafeteria mystery-meat bad.

They smell a lot like gunpowder.

Sometimes I can't help it, and I just fart without warning.

So, at my first day at regular school, we were having lunch in the lunch room when. . .

PFFFFFFTT!

All of a sudden, all of the kids ran away from me as fast as they could.

I tried to pretend it wasn't me.

But there was a little cloud of black smoke following me around that gave it away.

One kid lit a match to see what would happen.

No one has ever seen him since...

So, after that experience I couldn't find a school that could handle my...uh...problem.

Until we found a school for gifted mobs.

I think that was just a nice way of saying a school for kids with issues.

Like, there are a lot of Blazes, Endermen and Withers at this school.

And those guys have real issues.

But, my mom and dad said this school was perfect for me.

I didn't know why they said that.

Then after my first day, it totally made sense.

Here's a picture of Ms. Nilnose, my homeroom teacher.

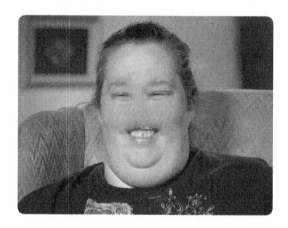

And then there's Principal Shortsnout.

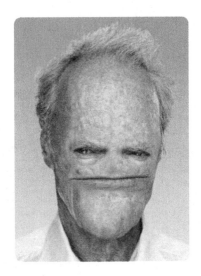

And then there's my Math teacher, Mr. Cheese.

Man, that guy can talk. . .

I wish I could go to the school in the village next to me, though.

But Villagers are mean.

I heard a rumor that most Villagers want to blow up Creepers.

I think it's because they probably think that we blow up their stuff up on purpose, too.

If I ever meet one, I want to tell them that Creepers are really nice but we just get real excited, thasss all.

But, I don't think they'll believe me.

Especially since a charged Creeper recently blew up a Villager's brand new house.

If you didn't know, a charged Creeper is a Creeper that was struck by lightning.

It doesn't happen a lot, but when it does, a charged Creeper blows up ten times bigger than a regular Creeper does.

So, I think my Uncle Sparks was passing by a Villager's house one day and then it started to rain.

Next thing you know, the Villager's house blew up.

Poor Uncle Sparks.

My dad always said he had an explosive personality.

Real hot-head that one. . .

Wednesday

Today my family went out to my favorite restaurant for dinner.

They have the best bean burritos you ever tasted.

Only thing I don't like about it is that it always smells like gunpowder.

Now, I think my family, The Creepers, are really cool.

Mom and Dad are okay, especially for parents.

I have an older sister named Ima, Ima Creeper.

And I have a younger brother named Seymour, Seymour Creeper.

We have a cool family although my older sister and little brother can be a pain sometimes.

We even started a family band.

We call ourselves The Creepers.

I play the guitar, Mom plays the tambourine, Dad plays the drums, and my sister Ima sings.

Seymour just plays his rattle.

It was a little hard to learn how to play our instruments, but eventually we got the hang of it.

You have to get real creative when you don't have any arms.

One thing I really like about my family is that we go on vacation a lot.

My favorite place to go is the jungle Biome.

I like it because I get to swing on trees and stuff.

Yeah, that took a lot of practice too.

We found an ocelot in the jungle Biome once.

We tried to take it home and keep it as a pet.

Yeah, that didn't go very well.

I think it's because I'm allergic to cat hair.

Every time I got around Oslow—that's what we called him—I kept sneezing and hissing.

So, we gave him to my Uncle Crackpot Creeper instead.

Looking back, I don't think that was such a good idea.

You see, my Uncle Crackpot started sneezing and hissing all over the place too.

Unfortunately, he's not with us anymore.

Neither is Oslow. . .

Speaking of pets, what I really want is a pet pig.

But my mom says that pigs don't get along with Creepers.

She says that there is too much history there.

Something about us being too much alike.

Honestly, I don't understand what she's talking about.

Thursday

Today, at school, I caught up with my best friends, who I hang out with all the time.

There's my neighbor, Harry Obrien.

But we call him Herobrine for short.

But I don't think he likes that name.

Every time we say it, the temperature in the room rises.

31

There's also my friend, Ed the Enderman.

He's really cool because he can teleport and stuff.

You just need to keep an eye on your things when you're around Ed.

Stuff tends to go missing whenever he's around.

And there's my friend Ned, Jed, and Fred.

He's a Wither. Or they're a Wither. I can never get that right.

They're great. But they talk a lot, though.

When one head stops talking the other one starts.

He could probably talk to himself for hours.

Now, our favorite game to play is a game called Hide and Sneak.

It's kinda like Hide and Seek except we have to sneak up and scare each other.

But no matter how much I play, I can never win.

Herobrine has a way of just sneaking up on me out of nowhere.

Ed, the Enderman, just vanishes before I can get really close to him.

And Ned, Jed, and Fred can always see me no matter what direction I come from.

My mom says I should stop playing with these guys.

She says they're a bad influence.

I just think she doesn't like me playing Hide and Sneak.

Something about Creepers not handling surprises very well.

Friday

Today I was running late for school, so I decided to ride the school bus instead.

My Mom told me not to ride on the school bus.

She said something about Creepers not doing well in enclosed spaces.

But today I decided I was going to try it.

As soon as I walked on the bus, I knew I was in trouble.

When I got on the bus, there was a huge sign in front of me that said. . .

**ABSOLUTELY NO FARTING
ON THE BUS!**

Oh man, it was too late to get off the bus so I had to find a way to keep from getting too nervous.

So I looked around to see who I could sit next to.

Most of the seats were taken, except for an empty seat next to an Enderman kid.

As I walked closer to him, I could tell he was a little different. I think it was the scar over his left eye.

"What are you staring at Noob?!" he said.

Oh boy, I started getting really nervous now.

So, I decided to avoid him and sit next to a Ghast girl.

I could tell she was really shy because she just sat there making cat noises.

After I sat down, I heard one of the kids sneeze behind us.

All of a sudden, the Ghast girl jumped up and started wailing and screaming all around the bus.

"Keep it down back there!" the bus driver yelled.

Finally, some other girls helped calm the Ghast girl down.

Then they spent the rest of the ride picking the boogers out of her hair.

I couldn't understand what all the fuss was about until I saw a couple of kids staring at my head.

You'd think because I was green, they would've blended in better.

Before we got to school, I could tell the mean Enderman kid was up to something.

When no one was looking, he took out a can of pumpkin stew and opened it.

I think we're not supposed to eat on the bus, but I didn't want to tattle on him.

But then he made a gurgling sound and dumped the whole can of pumpkin stew on the ground.

38

SPPPLLAAATTTT!!!

Then the whole bus went crazy.

All of sudden, the Enderman kid jumped up and yelled, "IT WAS THE CREEPER!"

"EWWWWWWW! CREEPER COOTIES!"

Everybody started looking at me and pointing their fingers.

Yeah, that was the last bit of motivation I needed to pull the pin off my butt grenade.

Then, when the smell hit them, all the other kids started throwing up.

By the time we got to school, the bus looked like there was an explosion at a cottage cheese factory.

Now I think I know why my Mom told me I shouldn't ride the school bus.

Saturday

Today, I went to a convention called Minecon so I could check out the new Minecraft toys that came out.

One of the things I like to do for fun is collect cool toys.

I'm almost finished collecting all the Minecraft action figures.

Though, I'm still having a hard time finding Herobrine.

Except, when I got to the convention, no one would talk to me.

I don't know why.

I would go up to people and say, "*Thasssss a very nice toy you've got there. . . It'd be a sssshame if anything were to happen to it. . .*"

And then they would run away.

I guess they didn't like my lisp.

. . .Or my farts.

I also like collecting music discs.

I keep a few with me all the time.

Mom says I shouldn't walk around with music discs in my pocket.

She says I may run into a gang of Skeletons.

Sunday

Now, the weirdest thing happened today.

A bunch of Zombies went crazy and took over the village next to my house.

My friend Zeke said his mom called it a Zombie Apocalypse.

I just thought they were having a sale on turquoise shirts or something.

...And I didn't even know Zombies had lips.

It was kinda weird because Zombies are usually really nice.

It wasn't like them to get all crazy and stuff.

But they were grunting and drooling and acting all uncivilized.

And it wasn't even dinnertime!

My Mom said that weird stuff like that always happens to kids at our age.

She called it puberty. . .whatever that means.

Weird stuff started happening to all my other friends, too.

Ned, Jed, and Fred started hurling skulls every time they sneeze.

Now, it wouldn't be so bad if they didn't blow everything up.

First time it happened, they were in the school bathroom and Fred had to sneeze.

Next thing we know, it was raining colored toilet paper.

Ed the Enderman started going through changes, too.

He started walking in his sleep.

It's not dangerous, though.

Although, one day my little brother went missing.

And the next day, we found him at Ed's house.

We still don't know how he got there.

I started going through changes of my own.

My neck is a little longer than it was a few weeks ago.

And I started to hover a little off the ground when I walk.

Comes in handy when I'm walking over puddles, though.

But the one that's really going through changes is my friend Herobrine.

His eye sockets started glowing in the dark all of a sudden.

And, sometimes when he gets mad, stuff just bursts into flames around him.

We were a bit creeped out at first.

Now, we just make him mad whenever we want to make s'mores.

47

Yum. . .

Monday

Today in writing class, Ms. Nilnose asked us to write about what we wished for most.

Yeah, she's always asking us to write about corny stuff like that.

But, after thinking about it for a while, I wrote down that I really wish they would find a cure for Creeper Spontaneous Combustion.

Because if they did, then I'd be able to do all the things that I really want to do.

Things like:

Ride on rollercoasters.

Do parkour.

Go skydiving.

Go Bungee jumping—though I came close to doing this on a dare once.

Play paintball.

Play dodgeball.

Play hopscotch.

Breakdance.

And be a contestant on American Idol.

Yeah, being a Creeper, I miss out on a lot of cool things in life.

But my real secret wish is to get a tattoo.

It would probably say Mom. . .or Mojang or something cool like that.

Now, you're probably wondering where I would put it.

On my butt. . .where else?

That's where all the other Minecraft mobs put it.

Plus, that way everybody can see it.

Tuesday

Today is the Fourth of July.

And, it's also my birthday.

My favorite part about the Fourth of July is the fireworks.

Now, Creepers make the best fireworks.

It's because of the gunpowder we use.

You see, we use the best gunpowder because it's all natural.

Now, I know what you're thinking. . .

And, the answer is yes. . .Creepers do poop gunpowder.

It makes great fertilizer and great fireworks.

Sweet!

We can make different color fireworks depending of the color of our gunpowder poop.

So, on the Fourth of July, we eat different foods to get the best colored fireworks.

We eat apples for red fireworks.

We eat pumpkins for orange fireworks.

And we eat golden apples for gold fireworks.

But, today I'm going to get really creative.

I'm going to eat a whole bag of Skittles, and my fireworks are going to be awesome!

Now, for my birthday, my mom made two cakes.

One for me...

And one for everybody else...

My mom also made me pumpkin pie because I really like eating pumpkins.

I mean, I can eat pumpkins in everything.

Pumpkin stew, pumpkin pie, pumpkin pudding, pumpkin cake. . .pumpkin everything.

My mom thought because I like pumpkin so much, she could trick me into eating my greens.

Didn't work. . .

I don't know why Mom wants me to eat my greens.

I'm already green enough so what do I need them for?

She says because they're green, they're nutritious.

Yeah, so are boogers but you don't see me eating those.

Blech!

Wednesday

Today after school, my Mom and Dad took us to my grandma and grandpa's house.

I think they said they had to go to a PTA meeting at my school.

Yeah, I didn't believe them.

I think they just snuck out to go scare some Villagers or something.

But, I really like visiting my grandparents.

My grandpa's name is Harry Creeper.

He looks a bit different than most Creepers.

He smells really funny, too.

Especially when he gets wet.

My grandma's name is Ada Creeper.

She's really nice.

She's actually from a Biome where they grow a lot of Ender Berries.

They say she ate too many Ender Berries when she was a kid and it turned her a different color.

Here's a picture of her from when we went on vacation. . .

She also makes the best purple fireworks I've ever seen.

On my mom's side, I have cool grandparents too.

But they travel a lot, so I don't see them much.

My grandpa's name on my mom's side is Major Creeper.

He was one of the first Creepers allowed in the Zombie army.

He works on the Bomb Squad.

But it's not what you think. He doesn't work with bombs.

He's more like a crash test dummy. . .

But for bomb squad practice.

My grandma is named Twilight Creeper.

She was a famous actress once.

They say she even had her own TV show.

But it got cancelled.

I heard she got replaced by ponies or something like that.

Thursday

Today I was thinking that if I could be like anybody in the whole world, I want to be like my favorite hero of all time, the Incredible Hulk.

He's awesome.

I imagine I'm the Incredible Hulk sometimes.

I imagine that I'm super strong, huge, and I can walk around barefoot like the Hulk.

Wait a minute. . . I am barefoot.

But I like how the Hulk jumps really far.

If I could do that, I would jump from one Biome to the next.

I could jump to grandma's house and get some pumpkin stew whenever I wanted.

Or if I fart, I could jump really far so no one would know it was me.

. . .And I wouldn't have to smell it.

My other favorite superhero is the Green Lantern.

I like him because he can make cool stuff with his ring.

If I had a ring like that I would use it to make a giant hand.

I would use it to wave my farts away real fast.

The other cool cartoon characters I like are:

Shrek

Kermit the frog

Green Giant

Green Arrow

Grinch

Yoda

Ninja Turtles

And Oscar the Grouch

They're real cool.

And they're greeeeeeen!

Friday

Today, some of the guys came over to my house for a sleepover.

We decided we were going to watch my favorite movie of all time called "Jeepers Creepers."

But I can only watch ten minutes of it because it's so scary.

I tried to watch the whole thing once.

But it was really hard peeking through my fingers.

I like movies because I like to imagine I'm the hero.

Then after the movie is over, I like to act it out in real life.

I think a lot of Creepers do that.

It's probably why they don't show any more Kung Fu movies on TV anymore.

Unfortunately, there aren't any Creeper action movies.

They did try to make a Creeper action movie once.

I think It was called "Final Detonation."

They started filming, but I heard they couldn't finish.

They ran into a lot of problems.

Something about the actors not coming back to work.

I guess Creepers weren't meant to be action stars.

. . .or stuntmen.

Saturday

When I woke up this morning, Herobrine, Ed, and Ned, Jed and Fred were already awake.

They were arguing about the one thing would they change in the next Minecraft update.

Then they asked me.

"Well, If I could, one of the things I would change in Minecraft is to take away a Creeper's spontaneous combustion effect," I said.

Actually, now that I think about it, I would give it to a Villager instead.

Let them deal with the stinky farts and having to always keep from getting excited.

Though, I would keep the colored gunpowder poop. . .it's just too cool.

The other thing I would change in Minecraft is I would make things a little more round around here.

Instead of square trees, I would make them into giant balls.

I would make them look like lollipops or something.

But don't get me wrong, I like squares.

Especially the watermelons. . .

Another thing I would change is that I would make the days a bit longer.

Since Minecraft days are only twenty minutes long, it's really hard to get anything done around here.

Also, the Zombie and Skeleton neighborhood kids can only come out for ten minutes every night.

Kinda makes it hard to make friends.

And, because the days go so fast, I'm a lot older than I look.

In your years, I'm only eleven years old.

But in Minecraft years, I'm about 315,569 years old.

Just call me "Gramps," why don't you.

The last thing I would change in Minecraft is give Creepers longer arms.

Creepers really do have arms.

But they're short and stubby, like our legs.

Makes it really hard to keep our clothes on.

Why do you think we walk around naked all the time?

But if I had arms I could finally shake hands with people I meet.

Normally, when I meet somebody, they stick out their hand for a shake.

I feel real dumb just standing there looking at their hand.

It's probably why Creepers have a reputation for being anti-social.

Sunday

Today, somebody was posting all kinds of crazy rumors about Creepers on Face-Mob.

Some of the things they uploaded were just downright mean.

Like, here's one that really bothered me. . .

I actually like cats.

I'm just allergic to them, thasss all.

Here's another one that's not even anatomically correct. . .

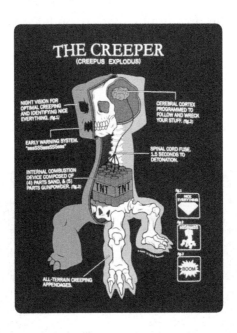

No, our brains are not connected to TNT.

At least that's what my mom said when I asked her about it.

But she did give me a weird look
once. . .when I told her I got the bubble guts.

Here's another one. . .

On second thought, this one is kinda true.

What can I say?

Creepers love hugs.

But this one, really?

Now, this is just wrong on so many levels.

Monday

Today, our 7th grade class went on a field trip to an abandoned Mineshaft.

And boy it was scary.

They had minecarts, and rails, and cobwebs.

And I don't like cobwebs.

When I get them on my face, I have a really hard time pulling them off.

As we were searching the tunnels, we found a chest with cool stuff in it.

Ms. Tibia, our science teacher, told us not to touch it.

But I think every kid left that place with a souvenir.

I tried to grab a diamond pick ax I found in there, but that didn't work out too well.

So, I took the next best thing. . .some cake!

Good thing is, if they search me they'll never find it.

Unless they find a pile of gunpowder with cherries in it.

The class went farther down the mineshaft to see if we could explore more stuff.

But I stayed behind because I felt my stomach rumbling.

So, I ducked behind a rock and let out a little toot so that nobody would notice.

But when I turned around, they were all gone.

Yeah, they noticed.

"Aw, man! Who took my stuff?!" somebody yelled.

Uh oh. I guess the owner of the chest came back.

But I don't know how. Nobody ever mines at night.

"Ewww! What's that smell?"

I guess he noticed, too.

"Man, that smells like rotten flesh, mixed with moldy cheese, mixed with fireworks," the stranger said.

I tried to keep quiet, but I was getting excited again.

HSSSSSSS. PFFFFT.

"Who's there?"

HSSSSSSS. PFFFFFFFFFFFFT.

"All right, I can hear you. And I can smell you, blech. Come out or I'm gonna throw this block of TNT at you."

TNT! Oh, man, I better come out before I really drop a bomb.

So, I came out from behind the rock.

"Ahhh! A Creeper!"

HSSSSSSS.

"Hey, wait a minute, you ate my cake?"

Wha? How did he know? I didn't even have any icing on my face.

"How did you know?

"Let's just say your farts smell like vanilla flavored gunpowder."

Wow, talk about embarrassing.

"Sorry about that. I didn't mean to eat your cake. It was just sitting there and it looked so good, thass all."

"Eh, don't worry about it. I'll just go back to the village later and get more."

"So, you're not mad?"

"Mad, no way. Because I found the biggest diamond you can imagine," the square-headed boy said as he pulled a big, shiny, bright diamond out of his pocket.

"Oooohhhhh prreeeecioussssssss," I said.

Then he gave me a really weird look.

"Ooooh Kay. Hey, what are you doing here anyway?"

"Well, I was on a field trip today but I lost my group."

"Well, I'm in a pretty good mood so I'll help you find them," he said.

"Thanks a lot!" I said, staring at the diamond as he put it in his pocket.

"So, what's your name?"

"My name is Jasper. Jasper Creeper. What's yours?"

"I'm Steve," he said.

Then, he reached out his hand for a shake.

But I just stood there. . .looking at it.

Monday, Later
That Day. . .

"**W**hat was your class doing in the mines, anyway?" Steve asked.

"Well, we were supposed to be studying Villagers and their weird customs. You know, like when Villagers just grunt instead of speaking, or why they have such long noses, or why they wear robes in the middle of the summer. . .stuff like that."

"You know, now that you mention it, that is weird."

"So today, we were doing a field trip to see where Villagers go all day. The cool part is that we keep finding chests full of really cool stuff. The other kids already found a ton of cool stuff they're taking back to school."

"Did you say chests? Oh no. . ."

I could tell by the look on Steve's face that either he was really mad, really constipated, or that something was wrong.

"What's up?" I asked Steve.

"Some Villagers booby trap their chest to make sure nobody steals their diamonds. If those kids open the wrong chest, then. . ."

Oh, man. I knew what that meant.

"Which way do you think they went?" Steve asked.

"I don't know. I think they said something about looking for a dungeon."

"Oh, I know where that is," Steve said. "It's really close. It's at. . ."

BOOOOOM!

Oh man. . .I think I better start looking for a new school.

Tuesday

Yeah, it's Tuesday already.

I told you days go by really fast in Minecraft.

Well, we finally found our class or what was left of them.

Just kidding.

The explosion didn't really hurt anybody.

Except one Enderman kid named Stan got a little hurt.

Stan has really sticky fingers.

You never know where your stuff is when Stan's around.

But I guess now we won't have to worry about that anymore.

The entire class was trapped in one of the dungeons.

The explosion caused a cave-in at the front of the entrance.

We could hear them through the rocks. But we couldn't get to them.

They even said they were trapped in there with a Spider monster spawner.

Well, that's when my hero turned to zero.

You see, I don't like spiders.

They give me the creeps.

I just get weirded out by how they crawl around with their little legs and how they sneak up on you and stuff. . .

And that hissing sound just drives me crazy.

"So, how are we going to get them out of there?" I asked Steve.

"I don't know. But we're going to have to do it soon. This place is really unstable."

All of a sudden, I started feeling wet.

But don't worry, I hadn't farted so I was safe.

"Hey, Steve, look!"

"There was water seeping out from the giant rocks that were covering the dungeon room.

"I think the explosion opened up an underwater lake," Steve said. "If we don't get them out of there, they're not going to last long."

Well at least it'll take care of the spider problem, I thought.

Naw, what am I thinking. We need to do something!

But, Steve and I tried everything.

Well, it's more like Steve tried everything.

I don't have arms, remember?

But nothing worked.

The water was rising higher and higher.

I could even hear the zombies moaning, the Skeletons clacking, and the Creepers hissing.

Which made me even more nervous.

Then I started hissing.

"Calm down, Jasper," Steve said. "We'll figure something out."

Then things got quiet.

"Awwww! What's that smell?!"

"Sorry," I said. "I'm nervous."

Then Steve tried to hold his breath.

"Now you know why my nickname in school is Silent but Deadly. . .and Under Thunder. . .and Barking Spider, which honestly really offends me, and. . ."

"Dude, you're a genius!" Steve said. Or that's what I think he said.

91

It was hard hearing him because he had his shirt over his big square head.

Steve grabbed his bag and started looking for something.

He pulled out a torch.

"What are you going to do with that?"

"Well, you ever heard of fart lighting?" Steve said with a creepy look on his face.

"Uh. . .no."

"Well, if we can fill this whole cave with your nasty smelling gunpowder farts that should give us enough gas to blow a hole in the doorway of the dungeon," Steve said.

"Won't it blow us up, too?"

Man, I wasn't sure if the rumors about Villagers were true. But this would be the perfect opportunity for Steve to start blowing up Creepers.

"Don't worry, we'll be safe if we hide in one of the other tunnels," he said.

"Oh, okay. . ." I think.

"So, go for it!" Steve said expecting something climactic.

"Go for what?"

"Dude, lay down some cheese."

"Cheese?"

"Yeah, drop an A-bomb"

"A wha. . .?"

"You know, break wind, squeeze cheese, throw an air biscuit, burn down the barn, beep your horn, blast the bazooka, exhume the dinner corpse, roar from the rear, step on a frog, get out and walk Donald, turn up the audio to eleven. . ."

"You want me to toot?!! I can't do it while you're watching. Besides, it only happens when I'm nervous or when I laugh. . .or when I get really excited."

Then I could see Steve's face light up like a Christmas tree.

All of a sudden, Steve stood up on a rock like he was going to give a speech.

"Hey, Jasper, did you hear the one about the Creeper that went to the doctor?" Steve said.

"Uh...no," I said, not knowing what to expect.

"Well, the doctor told the Creeper, 'I'm sorry but you suffer from a deadly disease and you only have ten to live.'

The Creeper said, 'What do you mean, ten? Ten what? Ten months? Ten weeks?!'

The doctor said, 'Nine...eight...seven...'"

"Tee, hee, hee..."

VRRRNNT!

"Hey, it's working!" I said. "Keep going, Steve!"

Then, Steve adjusted his imaginary bow tie and continued...

"One day a Witch asked her son, 'Paul, do you think I'm a bad mother?'

The son says, 'My name is Jim.'"

"Ha, ha, ha. . ."

BRRRTTT!

"Ha, ha, ha. . ."

BRRRTTT!

I could tell Steve was really trying to keep a straight face, but I think the smell was getting to him.

"Two Skeleton girls were fighting over a Skeleton boy. Then the Skeleton boy called the police.

The Skeleton boy said, 'Hey there are two Skeleton girls here fighting over me.'

The Policeman asked him, 'So. . .what's the problem?'

The Skeleton boy says, 'The ugly one is winning.'"

"HEHEHEHEHE!!!"

BRAAAHTHPPTPTPTPTPTT!

Cough, Cough, Cough.

"Come on, Steve, you can do this!" I said.

"Cough, okay!" Steve said.

"A teacher said to his Mob class one day, 'If you think you're dumb, please stand up.'

Nobody stood up, so the teacher said, "I'm sure there are some kids in this class that think they're dumb!"

Then Little Johnny the Creeper stood up.

The teacher said, 'Oh, Johnny! So, you think you're dumb then?'

Little Johnny replied, 'No, I just felt bad that you were standing by yourself.'"

"HAHAHAHAHAHA!"

FRR. . . FRR. . . FRRRRRR. . . RAMPOOOOOOOOAG. . . PPPPPPPPTTTTTTTTTTTTTTTT!

I think we had enough farts to blow up five dungeons.

Plus, Steve was turning a weird green color.

"He, he, he. . .Steve, I think we can stop now," I said.

"Hold up. I got one more," Steve said, trying to talk in between fainting spells.

"A Creeper's mom asked her son, "How was school today, Patrick?"

Patrick said, "It was really great, Mom! Today we learned about why Creepers explode."

The Creeper's mom said, 'Ooh, they teach really fancy stuff in school these days. What are you going to do at school tomorrow?'

Then Patrick said, 'What school?'"

"Hey, that's not funny," I said. "I have a cousin that happened to."

Well, we had everything we needed.

The whole mineshaft smelled like a Creeper Reunion at a chili contest.

And we needed to hurry because the water was almost reaching the top of the dungeon.

"Stand back, everybody!" Steve yelled between breaths.

So, Steve and I ran to the entrance of another mineshaft.

Then, he lit the torch and threw it toward the dungeon entrance.

And then. . .

KKKKAAAABBBBBOOOOOOMMM!!!!

A gush of water came rushing through the mineshaft, dragging all of us with it.

Finally, it stopped at the end of the mineshaft where we first found Steve's chest of stuff.

A few spiders hitched a ride on the tidal wave, too, which I didn't think was cool at all.

So, me and Steve saved my entire 7th grade class.

And, the kids were so grateful they gave Steve all his stuff back.

Except for the cake.

Yeah, that was gone. . .for good.

Wednesday

After our near-death experience in the Mineshaft yesterday, Ms. Nilnose asked me to write a paper about the one thing that I would want to let the world know about Creepers.

Well, after thinking about it for a while, this is what I wrote:

Dear World,

I wanted to write this paper to give you a little peek into a Creeper's life to help stop some of the rumors people have made up about Creepers.

Those rumors can really hurt, you know.

First of all, we don't purposely blow players up in Minecraft.

We just get really excited to meet you, thasss all.

And, we don't blow up your house when you're not looking.

Just don't leave sharp objects or cactus plants around your new house if you really care about it.

And no, we don't blow up your stuff on purpose. . .

Well, not all the time, anyway.

And, yes, Creepers have stubby arms and legs and we walk around naked all the time.

And, yes, Creepers have stinky farts and poop gunpowder.

And, yes, Creepers explode if we get too nervous or too excited.

But everybody has their quirks.

And ours just make us special, thasss all.

So, if you can look past all the weird quirks and our hazardous personality. . .

You'll realize that we're really warm and loveable inside.

And we really, really, really love hugs.

Find out What
Happens Next in...

Diary of a Minecraft Creeper Book 2

Coming soon. . .

105

If you really liked this book, please tell a friend. I'm sure they will be happy you told them about it.

Leave Us a Review Too

Please support us by leaving a review. The more reviews we get the more books we will write!

Check Out Our Other Books from Pixel Kid Publishing

The Diary of a Minecraft Creeper
Book Series

Get The Entire Series on
Amazon Today!

The Diary of a Minecraft Enderman
Book Series

Get The Entire Series on
Amazon Today!

Made in the USA
Monee, IL
28 May 2020